Then & Now
NOTTINGHAM

MIDDLE MARSH

Seventeenth and eighteenth-century houses at the foot of Drury Hill, *c.* 1900, showing a glimpse of Nottingham as it had been two centuries earlier. This was the heart of Broad Marsh with Drury Hill – the steep, narrow street on the right – once the only road into Nottingham from the south; it would have been the scene of countless altercations between the waggoners, horsemen and pedestrians jostling in the thoroughfare. This area is now the middle of the Broad Marsh Shopping Centre which opened in the early 1970s.

Then & Now
NOTTINGHAM

COMPILED BY DOUGLAS WHITWORTH

TEMPUS

Tempus Publishing Limited
The Mill, Brimscombe Port,
Stroud, Gloucestershire, GL5 2QG

ISBN 0 7524 1646 4

Typesetting and origination by
Tempus Publishing Limited
Printed in Great Britain by
Midway Clark Printing, Wiltshire

The Old Market Square in 1954. The huge traffic roundabout in the foreground was partly built on the site of the statue of Queen Victoria, which was transferred to the Memorial Gardens on the Victoria Embankment in 1953. The traffic on Long Row is being held up by a parade of the Boys' Brigade, watched by onlookers enjoying the evening sun. South Parade still contained a few eighteenth-century buildings including Farmers drapery store and the Savoy Café.

CONTENTS

Acknowledgements   6

Introduction   7

1.   The City Centre   9

2.   Around the Castle   29

3.   Broad Marsh   47

4.   Beyond the City Centre   63

5.   Work and Leisure   79

The art deco dining room in Boots D.10 building in 1935. The factory, prosaically known as the Wets Building, was designed by Sir Owen Williams in the early 1930s and was hailed as the new Crystal Palace. The building has withstood the test of time – it has now been completely refurbished and is Grade I listed.

ACKNOWLEDGEMENTS

I wish to thank Mrs May Sentance and Miss Dorrie Stevenson – the daughters of Frank Stevenson – for once again allowing me the use of their father's photographs. I am also grateful to the following for the loan of prints: Geoff Blore, The Boots Co. Plc, The City of Nottingham Local Studies Library, Clive Hardy, The Imperial War Museum, John Lock, John (Jack) Middleton, Nottingham Harmonic Society, Royal Mail, William Smalley.

I am also indebted to Dorothy Ritchie and the staff of the Local Studies Library for their unfailing kindness and assistance. My thanks are also due to the following for their help in the production of this book: Claire Hulland, Rose Lucas, Nick Lucy, Betty Matear, Richard Pike, Don Press, Peter Smedley, Terri Sweeney, Charles Towsey, Alan Trease. Finally, I should like to express my gratitude to my wife Margaret whose help and advice have been so greatly appreciated.

Introduction

A book of comparison photographs is obviously only of interest if there is a significant difference between the old image and the new one. This selection of pictures is a personal choice of Nottingham's buildings and scenes which have changed during the twentieth century. The photographs of Plumptre Hospital are perhaps the exceptions to the rule as, although superficially there is little difference between the two pictures taken seventy-four years apart, the building suffered severely from neglect and vandalism during the 1990s and restoration work has only begun recently.

Among these illustrations are numerous examples of missed opportunities by the City Corporation and by local companies. Drury Hill, which was demolished in 1969, could have been incorporated into the scheme to build the Broad Marsh Shopping Centre and would have rivalled the reconstructed streets of old shops in the Castle Museum in York. The lamented Black Boy Hotel would still be enhancing Long Row today if there had been sufficient consideration of the issues of conservation in the 1960s. Some of the buildings compared in this book will be remembered by many and those too young to have known them can see the changes which have occurred over the years.

The centre of Nottingham has undergone a series of transformations, interspersed with years when little alteration took place. The physical layout of the city centre is much as it has been for centuries but many streets were widened in the late nineteenth century. New office buildings and shops were then built on the sites of the old slum properties, giving the city its Victorian character, which it retained until after the Second World War.

The construction of the Victoria Railway Station in the late 1890s caused the demolition of a whole neighbourhood of old houses, over twenty public houses and the Nottingham Union Workhouse. The station, which remained for fewer than seventy years, is remembered with affection by many Nottingham people. Its clock tower, which was saved from destruction, is now almost dwarfed by the nearby Victoria Centre flats.

The First World War brought a halt to further changes in the city but in the 1920s Friar Lane was widened, with the consequent loss of Dorothy Vernon's dwelling – a medieval house built on the site of a Carmelite friary. Towards the end of the 1920s the Great Market Place was the scene of a great transformation when the Exchange was demolished, along with the warren of shops, stalls and public houses at the rear. A number of these buildings were regarded as picturesque, but in many cases were unfit for habitation and were no great loss.

The dazzlingly white Council House which replaced the Exchange came as a great shock to the citizens of Nottingham and it was some time before the new town hall became fully accepted. The loss of the covered market and the removal of the Goose Fair from the Market Place following the construction of the Processional Way caused a public outcry – but to no avail.

The inter-war years saw the demolition of most of the condemned houses occupying land to the south and east of the city centre. The property in the Broad Marsh area was the most congested and the censure of the Minister of Health in 1920 hastened the rehousing of its inhabitants. New housing estates were built by the Council in the north and west of the city, leaving a wasteland which was not to be fully utilized until the 1970s with the building of the Broad Marsh Shopping Centre.

At the outbreak of the Second World War all council house building ceased and was only resumed after the end of the war in 1945. Fortunately, Nottingham was not too severely damaged by enemy raids and the Corporation felt no urgency to plan and rebuild. When rebuilding in the city centre began again in the 1950s the first major project was the construction of Maid Marian Way from Canal Street to Chapel Bar. This was the first part of a proposed inner ring road which cut a swathe through some of Nottingham's oldest streets and saw the demolition of Collin's Almhouses on Friar Lane.

In 1967 the Victoria Railway Station was closed, effectively leaving Nottingham on a branch line. The vacated land and Broad Marsh were conveniently available when new-style shopping centres were being planned in Britain. Both of these developments, while popular with many people, have not improved the city skyline and it is proposed to enlarge the Broad Marsh Shopping Centre still further.

Following protests at the despoiling of the city centre in the 1950s and 1960s the Corporation took heed of public opinion and began a policy of conservation rather than wholesale destruction.

In the last decade, the old disused land of the Midland Railway and Boots Island Street site have begun to be redeveloped. Following the building of the Inland Revenue Centre and Magistrates' Courts near Wilford Road, the rest of the area has been modernized, with cafés and bars lining the Nottingham Canal. Further east on the site of the old Boots warehouses, new buildings have been erected and life is being brought back to the locality.

The Lower Parliament Street area is also being revived with the old Sneinton Wholesale Market now converted into retail outlets and the Ice Stadium being replaced by the National Ice Centre. The latter project is of major importance to Nottingham and particularly to Sneinton which had previously been ignored by the city authorities.

This selection of photographs gives the reader an opportunity to see some of the changes which have occurred in Nottingham in the twentieth century and to make their own judgement on them.

An election rally in Alfred Street Central in 1912. T.W. Dobson, the Liberal candidate, is addressing a crowd during the Nottingham East by-election caused by the resignation of Captain J.A. Morrison, the Conservative and Unionist Member of Parliament. The audience appears to be more interested in the photographer – while in the background a suffragette is speaking to a fringe group. The election resulted in a win by 1,324 votes for the Conservative and Unionist candidate, Sir John Rees.

The opening ceremony of the Goose Fair at the foot of Market Street in 1925. William Board, the Town Clerk, is reading the charter granting Nottingham the right to hold a fair in the Market Place. Originally a livestock and produce fair held after harvest time, it gradually changed into a pleasure fair with a national reputation. After the mayor, on this occasion Charles Foulds, had declared the fair open, he and his party would tour the site, riding on the 'horses' and trying their luck at the coconut shy before returning to the Exchange for a civic lunch.

Chapter 1
THE CITY CENTRE

The Great Market Place around 1900, before electric trams had made their appearance on the streets of Nottingham. In the foreground is a rank of hansom cabs and a wagon, which was still the general-purpose carrier. To the right, Brigida Capocci is standing behind her ice cream stall – she and her compatriot Mrs Solari were well-known ice cream vendors for many years. On the left is the entrance to the Talbot, a Victorian drinking palace, with extravagant decorations and statuary. Griffin and Spalding's department store, in the centre, was rebuilt in Portland stone in the 1920s, later becoming Debenhams. In the background is the Exchange, which had stood for almost 200 years and which was replaced in 1929 by the grandiose Council House.

The statue of Queen Victoria at the western end of the Market Place, *c.* 1910. The statue was unveiled with great ceremony by the Duchess of Portland in 1905 and was to remain there for almost half a century. In the background are some of the well-known shops of the time including Singer's Sewing Machines, Darby's glass and china store, Pearson Bros department store, Calvert's tea store and Hope Bros, the clothiers. All these businesses have now gone, Pearson's behind the statue perhaps being the greatest loss. After the closure of the shop in 1989 the premises remained empty for several years while major restoration work was carried out. The new shops occupying the building were the target of an arson attack in 1996 which gutted the whole of the interior and the renovation of the building had to be repeated.

A ngel Row in 1905. A row of eighteenth and nineteenth-century town houses converted mainly into business premises. On the left is Matthews & Co., tailors, with Hamel & Co., engravers and designers, on the top floor. The building to the right, one of the finest in Nottingham, is Bromley House, the home of the Nottingham Subscription Library since 1821. The house was built in 1752 by George Smith, grandson of the founder of Smith's Bank. In 1905, the top floor was occupied by the photographer, Wallace Edwin Middleton, whose family continued in business there until 1955 when they moved to premises in Regent Street. Beyond Bromley House is a cycle depot and J. Perry the jewellers. Today, the ground floor of Bromley House has been converted into shops but still houses the Nottingham Subscription Library on the first and second floors. Next door the cycle depot has been replaced by a mock-Tudor building and on the extreme right are the Odeon Cinemas: both structures are out of character with the remaining buildings on this stretch of Angel Row.

oose Fair in the Great Market Place, 1914. The fair was becoming more congested every year with the entire Market Place filled with roundabouts, sideshows and stalls and the overflow extending into the surrounding streets. The covered market normally held here was suspended and tram services were disrupted during the week of the fair. Prominent at the fair were the roundabouts of Collins who had been a fairground family for generations. The new sensation at the fair was the racing car ride but all the old favourites were here such as the 'horses' and 'racing cockerels'. In the foreground is the tent holding Bostock & Wombwell's menagerie which always attracted large crowds. To the right on Long Row is Lyon's Café and next to it The Picture House which opened in 1912 and advertised continuous performances

from 11.00 a.m. to 10.30 p.m. Both these buildings remain with different uses but the square has been transformed by a processional way, fountains and flowerbeds. The occasional roundabout returns to remind the older citizen of the great fair held here in the past.

The construction of the underpass at Chapel Bar in the 1960s. This was situated at the northern end of Maid Marian Way, then being extended to Derby Road. The Corporation's plans were for an express way to be built around the city centre but the controversy caused by the construction of Maid Marian Way resulted in the cancellation of this project. In the background is the Methodist Mission adjoining the Albert Hall – the Mission building has now been replaced by an office block. The traffic roundabout is a delight in the spring and summer, being full of colourful flowers and trees.

Upper Parliament Street in 1928, prior to the demolition of these properties and before the widening of the road. In the centre is Manchester Chambers, a Victorian building containing several small businesses all with notices advising customers of their imminent closure or removal. On the side wall are advertisements of popular products such as Oxo, Fairy Soap, Ino Flakes and Bass beer. This building was replaced in the 1930s by T. Cecil Howitt's Empire House for A.B. Gibson Ltd, wholesale provision merchants. In the German air raid of May 1941 this building was severely damaged but was rebuilt after the war. When Gibson's moved to Daybrook in 1962, Pearson's of Long Row acquired the building and extended the Parliament Street frontage. After Pearson's closed in 1989, the building was demolished to be replaced by Pearson House, a Benefits Agency Office. Next door is Edwards, one of many bars in the area and successor to the Three Crowns public house.

London theatres. Nottingham audiences had seen some of the greatest Victorian and Edwardian actors and actresses on its stage including Henry Irving, Ellen Terry and Sarah Bernhardt. Across Parliament Street is the Elite Cinema opened in 1921 and acclaimed as the finest picture theatre outside London. In the centre of the street is a police box and iron railings surrounding the steps leading to the underground toilets. Now the subway contains toilets, a newsagent's kiosk and a footpath beneath Parliament Street. The Theatre Royal, which was purchased by the Corporation in 1969, was completely restored without losing any of its character. The statue on the right represents Carmen and was sculptured by Hilary Cartmel and unveiled by Simon Rattle in 1989.

Theatre Square in 1922. On the left is the colonnade of the Theatre Royal, modelled on the style of the classical

The Empire Palace of Varieties in 1968, the year of its demolition. The theatre was built in 1898 on the site of the old Theatre Royal dressing rooms and gave twice-nightly shows until 1958 when it closed down. All the famous comedians of the day appeared here including George Robey, Harry Lauder, Will Hay and Tommy Handley but, with the spread of television in the 1950s, variety theatres declined in popularity and the closure of the Empire was inevitable. After the theatre was pulled down the site remained undeveloped for ten years until the Royal Concert Hall was built. This opened in 1982 and has proved a great success. In the background is the Newton Building of Nottingham Trent

University, the successor to the Trent Polytechnic. To the right is the recently renamed Turf Tavern public house.

The Old Corner Pin at the junction of Clumber Street and Upper Parliament Street in 1991 just after its closure. A well-known Nottingham hostelry, the inn was originally called the George and later became the Horse and Groom. Since the closure of the Old Corner Pin, alterations have caused the building to lose all its character. After becoming a Disney store, for a while it was a fast food outlet and it has now reopened as a branch of Etam's fashion store. This road crossing is always busy as it is on the route between the city's two major shopping centres.

A rear view of the Natwest Bank on Thurland Street in 1988. This sight was possible for a time when the building at the corner of Clumber Street and Pelham Street was demolished. The building was designed by Watson Fothergill in 1882 for the Nottingham & Notts. Bank and has a façade resplendent with architectural detail. The round banking hall is notable for its stained glass windows and fine sculptures. The tall tower in the background with its four turrets serves a dual purpose, being decorative and also containing the bank's ventilation system. This corner of Clumber Street and Pelham Street is now occupied by a building housing a branch of the Alliance & Leicester.

shops. After the success of his Goose Gate shop, Jesse Boot opened a branch nearer the town centre in Pelham Street in 1893 and during the next few years made several alterations to the shop. His ambition, however, was to build a completely new department store and this became possible in 1903 when the Corporation cleared High Street of all its old properties. A.N. Bromley, an architect who was to be widely used by Jesse Boot, designed this building which incorporated both a café and a library as well as gift, toiletry and chemist departments. This Boots shop closed in 1972, since when the building has been occupied by a number of small firms. With the pedestrianization of much of the city centre, shopping has become easier, with only the occasional vehicle troubling passers-by.

Boots shop at the corner of Pelham Street and High Street in the 1930s. This was Boots premier store and the forerunner of all the company's major

High Street in 1929, as busy then as it is now. On the right is Boots the Chemists and at the corner of Long Row and Clumber Street is Skinner & Rook the grocers and wine merchants. The latter shop was well known for its freshly ground coffee, hampers of food and fine wines. The business was started by Mr Skinner in 1844 and joined by Mr Rook in 1860. The shop closed in 1955 when Skinner & Rook moved to Maypole Yard and this building was demolished. The first car on the right is a Morris Minor followed by a Bullnose Morris. The Long Row and Clumber Street corner now has an office block with branches of national shops on the ground floor.

Long Row East in 1966. This street had numerous buildings of individuality with the Black Boy Hotel as its centrepiece. The hotel started life as a coaching inn but was rebuilt in 1887 by Watson Fothergill in a North German style. In 1897 he altered and extended the hotel and for almost three-quarters of a century it was host to a multitude of guests and was known all over the country. This stretch of Long Row possessed several shoe shops, Sodens the furriers, Sands the milliners and Meakers the tailors. When the Black Boy Hotel was needlessly demolished in 1970 the statue of Samuel Brunt, whose ancestor bought the land around 1577, was removed from the façade and taken to St Peter's Church, East Bridgford. To replace the hotel, a faceless multiple store was built, with the only concession to tradition being the colonnade along Long Row.

The Flying Horse Hotel, The Poultry, in 1900. The hotel bears the date 1483 and stands upon the site of the house which the Plumptre family erected when they came to Nottingham in the thirteenth century. Although much restored, it still retained the appearance of an Elizabethan coaching inn and in the past was known as the Travellers Inn. On the right is J. & A. Kirk's Midland Bonnet Emporium, whose windows are filled from top to bottom with articles for sale. Today this stretch of The Poultry bears only a slight resemblance to the early years of the twentieth century. The Flying Horse is now a shopping arcade with a mock-Tudor façade which is a copy of the Rose & Crown at Saffron Walden. A

link with the past is the figure of Pegasus, the steed of Greek mythology, above the entrance to the arcade.

Bridlesmith Gate in 1921. The building in the foreground was already 200 years old when, in 1760, John Dann established his cooked meat business here. This Tudor house was one of the last to remain in the city, being demolished in 1945. Beyond is J.W. Asher the hatter, the Ashbourne Café and King John's Chambers. The latter is the site of the Rose Tavern, the eighteenth-century haunt of recruiting officers. Bridlesmith Gate, like many other old Nottingham streets, is named after the tradesmen who carried out their work here. Nowadays, modern buildings have replaced the old structures with no visual improvement.

Bridlesmith Gate from Drury Hill, *c.* 1930. In the Middle Ages this narrow street was the main road into the town from the south and would have been crowded with vehicles and pedestrians. Later, the street became noted for its fine shops where upper floors overhung the pavement. The building on the left is the office of Sun Fire & Life Insurance Co. and on the right is Noble & Co. who, besides being garment cleaners, repaired shirts, stockings and underwear. Bridlesmith Gate is still busy although no wider and is now a precinct with trendy shops.

Wheeler Gate, *c.* 1928. This is a street of mainly Victorian buildings with many businesses unknown to the younger citizens of Nottingham. On the corner of Hounds Gate is Vernon Heaton, advertising London suitings and next door is Alexandres, then a well-known outfitter. Beyond are two popular cafés, the Savoy and Morley's, and further up Wheeler Gate is the Oriental Café – none of which have survived. On the opposite side of the street is the Horse & Groom, which dates from the seventeenth century, and beyond is the Canadian Fur Co. In the right foreground a traffic policeman is standing on his box, with only light traffic to direct. This street is no longer the road to the south from the city centre. In the recent photograph, tall office blocks fill the sky but trees have been planted to soften their impact.

St Peter's Square, *c.* 1895. This was the terminus for horse-trams, which ran to London Road and Trent Bridge. The services were run by the Nottingham & District Tramway Co. which started in 1878 and was superseded in 1897 by the Nottingham Corporation. On the left is Alexander's, advertised as the Great Clothier, and across Exchange Walk is Marriott Bros, ironmongers, who were to remain for another half century. Beyond is the Eight Bells public house which was used for a scene in the film *Saturday Night and Sunday Morning* shortly after its closure in 1959. The new building on the site is a branch of the Nottingham Imperial Building Society.

Lister Gate in 1950. This was an area with some of the largest cash-trade shops in the city. On the left are the art deco buildings of F.W. Woolworth & Co. and British Home Stores with Marks & Spencer in the distance. The Walter Fountain is on the extreme left and due for demolition. The fountain was built in 1866 by John Walter MP in memory of his father, also John Walter MP, the proprietor of *The Times*. Beyond the fountain is the Sawyers Arms, an eighteenth-century inn which was also shortly to be pulled down. With the planting of the trees in this precinct the view towards the Council House has been blocked. A small fountain has been placed at the entrance to the Broad Marsh Shopping Centre as a reminder of the original edifice.

Jessamine Cottages in 1923. These cottages in Castle Road were originally the workhouse for the parish of St Nicholas and date from 1729. When the workhouse moved in 1815 to Butt Dyke, later renamed Park Row, this building was converted into separate cottages. Although perhaps not too comfortable for the occupants, the cottages were a picturesque sight from the castle walls. When the People's College of Further Education was planned in the 1950s, these cottages and several other old properties were demolished.

Chapter 2

AROUND THE CASTLE

Castle Gate in the 1930s. This road possessed some of the most important and attractive houses in Nottingham. The buildings on the immediate right are eighteenth-century dwellings and beyond is Newdigate House, which was built around 1675 and named after the Newdigate family who acquired it in 1714. When Maid Marian Way was constructed in the late 1950s Castle Gate was bisected with the loss of the first two houses on the right. Fortunately, Newdigate House was spared but there is now a stark contrast between it and the adjoining modern office block.

The entrance to Nottingham Castle in 1949. The gatehouse contains the remaining fragments of the ancient castle, but these were mostly hidden when it was restored in 1908. The grounds of the castle have always been popular with citizens and visitors, being only a short walk from the Old Market Square. The view over Nottingham was then unspoilt by tall office buildings and multi-storey car parks – the Council House dominating the skyline. Now, City House on Maid Marian Way and the Pearl Assurance building block the view towards the city centre. The photographer in the foreground of the recent picture has her camera trained on a fashion model with the castle as a backdrop.

The Meadows viewed from the castle in 1949. The near distance is filled with factories and warehouses and beyond are the terrace houses built in the late nineteenth century. In the left foreground is Viyella House, designed by Frank Broadhead for William Hollins & Co. in the early 1930s. The building was used as a factory and an office for the company's spinning and weaving business until 1961 when they moved their operations to London. Subsequently, it fell into decline until the James McArtney Partnership rescued it and completely renovated the building, now known as Newcastle House. The land adjoining the Nottingham Canal has now been acquired by the Inland Revenue for their innovative modern building. This area of Nottingham has now been revitalized with old warehouses restored and distinctive new buildings erected.

Castle Boulevard and the muddle of factories and railway warehouses viewed from the castle in 1923. One of the oldest established firms of the area is Gunn & Moore, the cricket bat manufacturers, who were established in 1885 by William Gunn and T.J. Moore. They are one of the few firms that occupy the same premises in both photographs – their name can be seen on the roof of their factory in the centre of the picture. In the middle distance on the left is one of the offices of the new Inland Revenue complex. Occupying the railway land are new warehouses and beyond is the Royal Ordnance – successors to Cammell Laird – known locally as the gun factory.

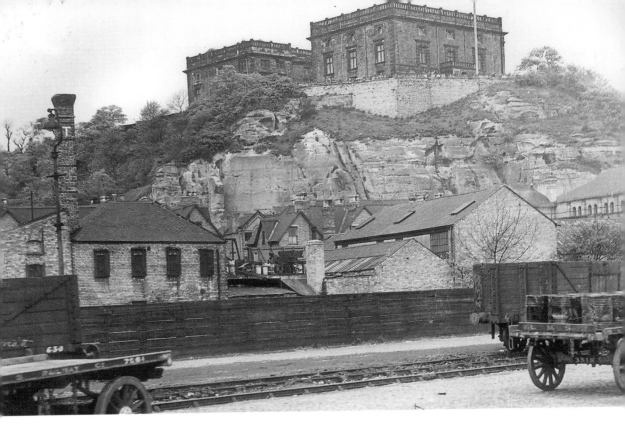

The castle seen from the London, Midland & Scottish Railway sidings in 1925. Until the middle of the nineteenth century this was meadowland which was regularly flooded by the River Trent and each spring was carpeted with masses of blue crocuses. The first railway line was laid here in 1839. The inaugural train journey went from Nottingham to Derby and was watched by thousands of spectators along the line. Nottingham Castle, standing prominently on the sandstone rock, is probably a great disappointment to visitors to Nottingham who expect to see a Norman fortress. The modern architecture of the Inland Revenue building in the later photograph is in striking contrast to the Italianate mansion in the background.

The city centre from the Viyella factory on Castle Boulevard in the early 1950s. In the immediate foreground are the premises of the Corporation Water Board and beyond is the Trip to Jerusalem and the seventeenth-century houses of Brewhouse Yard. In the centre of the picture is St Nicholas' Church School which was demolished in 1956 together with the remaining old houses in Broad Marsh. Today, this land is occupied by the People's College which blocks the view towards the centre of the city. The Council House, from this viewpoint, now stands incongruously amid the concrete tower blocks.

Broad Marsh from the castle walls in 1968. The demolition of the shops on Carrington Street was about to begin in preparation for the building of the Broad Marsh Shopping Centre. On the left is St Nicholas' Church, which was built around 1680 after the earlier church was pulled down on the orders of Colonel Hutchinson during the Civil War. In the distance, appearing almost joined, are the High Pavement Unitarian Chapel and St Mary's Church. Today the view is spoilt by the unsightly roof of the People's College and the Broad Marsh Shopping Centre. The churchyard of St Nicholas' is a small oasis in the middle of the modern architecture.

Castle Road in 1928. In the past this road was called Gillyflower Hill or July Flower Hill after the flowers found growing here. The caves in the castle rock are used for storage purposes, which has been their role for centuries. The massive walls above were restored in the early twentieth century when the gatehouse was rebuilt. Nowadays, Castle Road is a quiet backwater with more than its fair share of parked cars. On the right of the street, Severn's building has been relocated here and Watson Fothergill's Mortimer House is a delight. In the distance, beyond Friar Lane, the Rutland Hotel and Forte Crest Hotel can be seen.

The open aspect of the castle from the wasteland at the bottom of Castle Road in 1956. This was the year when St Nicholas' Church School on the right was demolished. The school was built in 1859 and closed in 1912, subsequently being used as a parish hall. The streets in this area, filled with tightly packed houses, were named after the participants in a tale of treachery and intrigue which took place in Nottingham Castle. In 1330 Edward III and his conspirators entered the castle where they arrested Roger Mortimer, the lover of Edward's mother Isabella, thus leaving behind an enduring legend. Today, there is only a glimpse of the castle through the car park of the People's College.

The Trip to Jerusalem around 1950, proudly proclaiming itself as the oldest inn in England. Nestling in the castle rock, it is supposed to be the inn where crusaders refreshed themselves on their journey to the Holy Land. The story has now been discounted but there has been an alehouse here since the Middle Ages. The present building dates from the eighteenth century when it was known as the Pilgrim. Today, the inn is still a tourist attraction with its bars cut out of the sandstone and a chimney extending vertically into the castle rock. The signpost on the left in the modern photograph still points to the Canal Museum which has unfortunately now been closed.

The seventeenth-century Royal Children inn at the corner of Castle Gate and St Nicholas Street in 1924. The story of the children of Princess Anne, daughter of James II, lodging here in 1688 is a myth. The princess fled to Nottingham Castle for safety during the Glorious Revolution but at that time had no living offspring. The whalebone hanging above the entrance is genuine and a relic of the days when whale oil first supplanted candles for lighting. The inn was demolished in 1933 and a mock-Tudor replacement was then built. The shoulder blade of the whale, after hanging outside the inn for centuries, is now kept in a glass case inside the building.

Castle Gate, around 1950, before Maid Marian Way cut a swathe through these old buildings. On the left are the wrought-iron railings of Newdigate House and two seventeenth-century houses followed by a Georgian town house. To the right is a temperance hotel with, adjoining it, St Nicholas' Rectory, which was designed by Watson Fothergill in 1886. The later photograph shows how Maid Marian Way has bisected Castle Gate, replacing old structures with modern buildings of little style.

Newdigate House, Castle Gate, in the 1920s when it had multiple occupation. The house is alternatively called Marshal Tallard's house after its famous resident. The distinguished French soldier lived here for several years after he was captured at the Battle of Blenheim in 1704. During the twentieth century the house was used for a variety of purposes including a girls' school, ballroom, armoury, dancing school and canine clinic. In 1966 the building, which was then dilapidated, was restored and became the home of the Nottingham & Notts. United Services Club, now called the Nottingham Club. The plaque outside the house refers to Marshal Tallart, which is considered to be the French spelling of the name. This gracious corner of Nottingham, in the heart of the city, is a peaceful retreat for contemplation.

The Salutation Inn, *c.* 1910. This inn is one of Nottingham's oldest public houses, although its overhanging roof suggests it was built in the sixteenth century rather than 1240 which is quoted on its walls. Beneath the inn are a series of rock caves which are of greater antiquity than the building itself. The caves were excavated over 800 years ago and consist of what is considered to be a dormitory, common house, a well, guardroom and a larder. During the coaching days the inn had a sinister reputation when it was much frequented by the 'gentry of the road' – the highwaymen. In 1956 the Salutation was restored and extended but today still gives the impression of a sixteenth-century tavern.

The junction of Friar Lane and Spaniel Row in 1922. The house on the corner was once owned by Sheriff Reckless who, in 1649, was converted by George Fox, the founder of the Society of Friends. The Quaker was given shelter here after his imprisonment for disturbing a service in St Mary's Church. Parked outside the house is a Rover 8 motorcar with its spare wheel and battery on the running board. During the road widening scheme of the 1920s a number of historical buildings were demolished including Dorothy Vernon's medieval house. These were replaced by anonymous office blocks.

Spaniel Row looking towards Friar Lane in 1921. The church on the right was built in 1737 for the Society of Friends but in 1847 it became the Catholic Apostolic Church. In 1867 Copestake, Moore & Crampton, the lace manufacturers, bought the church and used it for religious services for their employees. The adjoining house was once the property of James Huthwaite, who was three times the Mayor of Nottingham in the middle of the eighteenth century. The building in the background in Friar Lane is the Friends Adult School. None of these buildings have survived, being replaced by modern characterless offices.

The Broad Marsh bus station in 1968. While a decision on the long-term future for Broad Marsh was made, the land was used for a number of purposes including fairs, exhibitions and a bus station. During this period, the Victorian buildings of Weekday Cross and the Lace Market were visible from Broad Marsh. On the right is the High Pavement Unitarian Chapel and beneath it is the old High Pavement School which was built in 1805 and closed in 1895.

Chapter 3
BROAD MARSH

Severn's on Middle Pavement in 1964. This famous establishment was founded by John and James Severn in 1735 when they began a wine importing business here. This building, which was originally a merchant's house, is one of the oldest domestic properties in Nottingham. During the nineteenth century, Severn's extended into the adjoining building when their Gentleman's Eating and Dining House had a high reputation. In 1956 the fifteenth-century building was restored but the property was not to remain here much longer as it was dismantled in 1969 and moved to Castle Road. The replacement for Severn's is a bland structure with a wine and spirit shop on the ground floor.

Middle Pavement in 1969. The Georgian house which Severn's the wine and spirit merchants previously occupied had already been demolished, but the fifteenth-century wooden-framed building which adjoined it was waiting to be dismantled. When the plans for the construction of the Broad Marsh Shopping Centre were announced, there was an outcry at the proposal to demolish these buildings and also Drury Hill, but the protests had little effect. The medieval building was, however, reprieved and after being taken down it was re-erected on Castle Road. Low Pavement still retains some distinguished buildings including the eighteenth-century Vault Hall on the left. This street is now pedestrianized with automatic car barriers controlling entry for permit holders only.

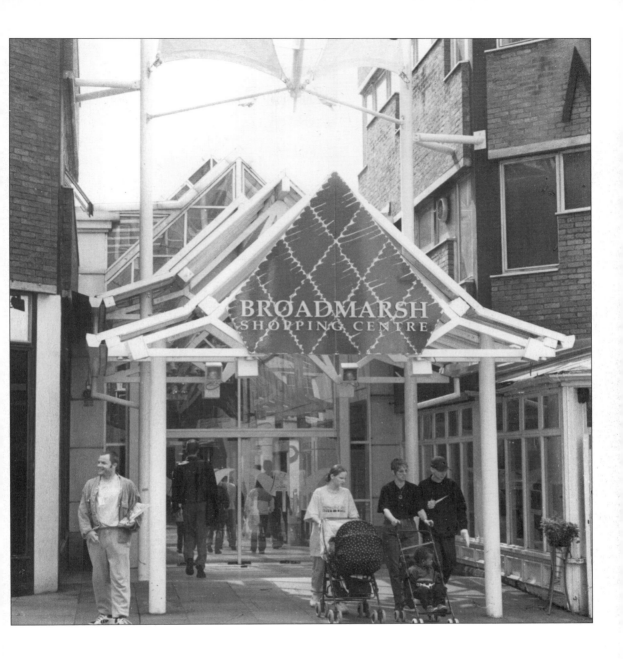

Drury Hill in 1964. This street was originally called Vault Lane after the huge rock cellars beneath the houses at its junction with Low Pavement. Around 1620 the street was renamed Drury Hill after Alderman Drury who then occupied Vault Hall. In the Middle Ages this street, although narrow, was an easier climb than Hollow Stone and until the seventeenth century this was the principal entry into the town from the south. Despite protests the buildings in this street were demolished in the late 1960s and the thoroughfare was submerged within the Broad Marsh Shopping Centre. This entrance to the shopping centre, known as Drury Walk, leads to an escalator at the foot of which a series of caves have been opened as a tourist attraction.

Long Stairs in 1913. This was one of the ancient routes from High Pavement down to Narrow Marsh. Halfway down the steps on the left is one of the fig trees which grew from the cliff face and which, despite the conditions, managed each year to leaf and fruit. Behind the wall on the left is Malin Hill, a path which leads down to Plumptre Square. In the distance is St Patrick's Church, which opened in 1880 and was a place of worship for 100 years, closing in 1979. When the slum property was cleared from Narrow Marsh in the 1930s, Long Stairs were closed, the steps being considered too dangerous. Today, only the iron gate and a few broken steps remain as a reminder of this medieval stairway.

M alin Hill in 1988. This bridle path from the old town, surrounding St Mary's Church down to the Meadows, is probably the oldest route out of Nottingham to the south. The hill is named after George Malin who lived here at the beginning of the fourteenth century. In 1525 Sir Thomas Willoughby founded and endowed a bede house here for five poor widows. This right of way has been preserved, although the buildings at the foot of the hill have all been replaced. The Town Arms public house on the left has now been supplanted by offices.

Short Stairs in 1989. This is another route from the escarpment of the old town down to the Meadows. These steps plunged directly to the foot of Malin Hill but wheeled traffic was obliged to use either Hollow Stone or Malin Hill. New buildings have been erected on this hillside – during the excavations, numerous caves were uncovered revealing pottery, clay pipes and other artefacts.

Leen Side, later renamed Canal Street, viewed from Malin Hill in the 1930s. Most of the slum dwellings were demolished by this time and new council houses built, but some old houses remain in the foreground. At the junction of London Road and Canal Street is a YMCA hostel and, to the right, the Globe Electrical Co. with three firemen's cottages adjoining it. The building surmounted by a cupola is the Leen Side police station and mortuary and next to it is the Council School for Infants. The police station is now the night shelter of the Nottingham Help the Homeless Association and the school, renamed the Sheriff's Lodge, is now the venue for medieval banquets. The old buildings towards London Road have been replaced by a traffic island. The building on the nearside of Canal

Street in the modern photograph is the extension to the Plumptre Almshouses, opened in 1959. The decline in demand for accommodation caused the closure of the almshouses in 1998, ending over 600 years of charitable work in the city.

Boots Island Street works from Malin Hill in the 1930s. The area derived its name from the virtual island created by a spur of the Nottingham Canal. Jesse Boot began manufacturing herbal remedies in his Goose Gate shop but in the early 1880s he leased three rooms in Elliott's lace-thread doubling factory in Island Street. By 1892 he had taken over the whole cotton mill and established his general office here. Jesse gradually bought more small factories and houses in the area and in 1914 he built his own factories on the site. The church in the foreground is the Roman Catholic Church of Our Lady and St Patrick, built in 1880 at a cost of £6,000 from designs of Evans and Jolly. As can be seen in the later photograph, none of these buildings remain – the church was pulled down in 1979 and the Island Street site is being converted into a business park.

Boots Island Street warehouses in 1969. These buildings were originally built as factories in 1914 and in the First World War were used to manufacture a range of goods for the troops. Boots were also responsible for the bulk of saccharin production in the country – this had previously been imported from the Continent. When the Boots site opened at Beeston in the late 1920s, these buildings were converted into warehouses. In 1996 they were demolished, ending over a century of Boots association with the area. Now a business park is being developed on the thirteen-acre site. The first building to be completed was the BBC Centre and there are plans for a hotel on the bank of the canal.

Plumptre Hospital in 1925. This was built in 1823, to a design of Edward Staveley, on the site of its predecessor. John Plumptre, a descendant of the founder of the charity, laid the foundation stone. The almshouses were established by John de Plumptre in 1392 to support thirteen poor widows and two priests. To commemorate the rebuilding of the hospital the area was renamed Plumptre Square, although the sign on the building reads Poplar Street. The building ceased to be almshouses in 1991 when the last occupant moved to new almshouses on Canal Street – these also belonged to the charity. The original property has remained empty since then – only recently has restoration work been completed converting this building into offices.

The Lace Market from Plumptre Square in 1988. William Allen's old stationery factory is on the right, occupied by Top Knot hairdressers. The white building in the centre is the Town Arms public house, which was closed after a fire that seriously damaged the upper floors. In the background are lace warehouses and factories lining Hollow Stone. The building on the left surmounted by a turret was Louis Trivett's lace-net factory, one of the many buildings constructed in the district as warehouses or factories in the second half of the nineteenth century. In recent years new office blocks have been erected here and during the construction several large caves were discovered, revealing much material of archaeological interest.

The canyon of Hollow Stone lined with lace factories in the 1930s. This route to the south from the medieval town was difficult and until 1740 the road was only wide enough for one carriage at a time. Trivett Square, on the right, leads to Short Hill and the steep steps of Short Stairs. The public house at the foot of Hollow Stone is Horne's Castle, notorious for one of its residents who was hanged for murder in 1759. For many years afterwards the house was called Old Horne's Hall. The modern photograph shows a twentieth-century road hazard – resurfacing of the highway. In the background is Manvers Court, a block of council flats in Sneinton.

Canal Street in 1988. The Narrow Boat public house in the centre was in the last few years of its life, closing down in 1996. This inn is a reminder of the heyday of the country's canals. In the background is the British Waterways building, originally the Trent Navigation warehouse, awaiting a new function. The whole area has now been regenerated with old warehouses converted into a series of bars and cafés. The Bar Risa and Jongleurs Comedy Club now occupy part of the British Waterways building along with the Fitness First Health Club. The *Nottingham Evening Post* moved in 1998 from their old Forman Street building into the new offices on the right, while on the left is a British Telecom office.

The Nottingham Canal in 1929. At this time it was still a working canal with barges constantly on the move or being loaded and unloaded. Giant motor barges were plying between Hull and Nottingham but horse-drawn barges could still be seen. This stretch of water between Carrington Street and Wilford Road was always full of activity – the barge on the right is being unloaded by a father and his small son. The modern picture shows a much more peaceful scene with only pleasure boats in sight, although dredgers are occasionally seen. The far side of the canal has been transformed with old warehouses converted into bars and restaurants. A footbridge has also been built to connect the two banks of the canal, the left bank of which is the site of the new Magistrates' Courts.

enton Lodge, *c.* 1920. The lodge was built as an entrance gate to Wollaton Hall in 1823 by Jeffry Wyatt, later Sir Jeffry Wyatville. Originally named Beeston Towers, it was built in the same style as the Prospect Room of the hall. When the Nottingham Corporation bought Wollaton Hall and estate in 1924, part of the land was sold for housing development, leaving the lodge isolated from the hall. In the 1930s the lodge was occupied by a police constable and his family, and later, park workers were housed here. After a period when the lodge was used as offices, it has now been sympathetically restored as a home with the central arch incorporated into the living accommodation.

Chapter 4
BEYOND THE CITY
CENTRE

The entrance to the General Cemetery, Canning Circus, in 1928. The cemetery was opened in 1837 at a cost of £6,000, the money being raised by a company of shareholders. The cottages in the terrace were built between 1837 and 1840 in what was described at the time as 'Grecian style with Italian finish'. They are not strictly almshouses but cottages, built by the Freemen's Rights Committee for senior freemen and their widows. The cottages were renovated and modernized in 1977-79 when the chimneys were reduced to their original height. This area has always been associated with interments as the bodies of suicides were buried at these crossroads in the past.

The Bluecoat School, Mansfield Road, in 1910. The school was founded in 1706 for the education of sixty boys and twenty girls, the first premises being in St Mary's Gate. Pupils were all issued with a suit of clothing on admission and children who failed to continue in school for at least a year were stripped of their uniforms. In 1723 the school moved to a new building on High Pavement where it remained until 1853. T.C. Hine designed the Mansfield Road school in the Elizabethan style with gables and mullioned windows – the statues of a girl and boy in traditional school uniform were placed in niches in the front of the building. The school continued in use until 1967 when a modern school was built in Aspley Lane.

Today, this building still retains the statuettes, although minus the belfry, and is the home of the International Community Centre.

The Nag's Head, Mansfield Road, in 1955. This was an old coaching inn which dates back to the fifteenth century. In the days when hangings took place on Gallows Hill, near the present-day site of St Andrew's Church, the execution procession paused here for the condemned prisoner to have a last drink – paid for by the landlord. The posters beyond the inn advertise John Gilbert in the play *Slightly Used* at the Theatre Royal and George Formby in a revue at the Empire Theatre. The Nag's Head is now a convivial place for a rest on the way up Mansfield Road.

Mansfield Road looking north from the roof of the Victoria Centre flats in 1988. The old Great Central railway tunnel on the right was blocked up when the Victoria Railway Station was pulled down in the late 1960s. With forethought this line would have been the ideal route for a tram system through the heart of Nottingham. On the skyline is the prominent church of St Andrew, built in the French Gothic style in 1871. Today a multi-storey car park and a coach station occupy the old railway cutting and the untidy buildings beyond have been replaced by new blocks of offices.

The view south from the roof of the Victoria Centre flats in 1973. In the foreground is the expansive roof of the Central Market which had recently closed. After almost half a century, Nottingham folk had become accustomed to the market in Glasshouse Street and were initially unhappy at the move to the Victoria Shopping Centre. Beyond, to the right, is the Lace Market, although very few of its buildings were then devoted to the manufacture of lace. On the left, appearing like a ship, is the Post Office sorting office on Huntingdon Street and in the background are the tower blocks of flats in Sneinton. The later photograph shows new offices and houses occupying the land where the Central Market once stood.

Hockley Chapel, Goose Gate, in 1931. The chapel was opened by John Wesley in 1783 and it was here in 1788 that he preached his last sermon in Nottingham. The building was sold to the Primitive Methodists in 1839 and they continued to worship here until 1937. The building was subsequently occupied by Ideal Homes, a furniture store, and later by the Nottingham Sewing Machine Company. In 1959 the façade was completely altered and there is now little evidence of the building's religious connections; the patrons of the Olympic House of Fitness are perhaps unaware of the place in history which it holds. In the 1930s the bargain-price shops in this area attracted customers from the Bottoms and beyond. After a period of decline, this district has now been revived.

Wool Alley, *c.* 1900. This street of stockinger's cottages ran between Woolpack Lane and Barker Gate, one of the many alleys in the district. The entrance to the street was through a low passage and this enclosure formed a little world for the young girls in the picture. Bowler Bros, who occupied the building in the left background, were machine and pattern makers – one of many small companies allied to the lace trade. Wool Alley disappeared in the slum clearances between the two world wars and the buildings which replaced it have now also been demolished. In their place is the main arena of the National Ice Centre, the later photograph showing its construction.

oots Print Services, Lower Parliament Street, in 1988. This art deco building was constructed in 1939 for R. Cripps & Son as a garage and car showroom but was requisitioned by the Auxiliary Fire Service at the outbreak of the Second World War. In the blitz of May 1941 this area suffered a great amount of damage and the emergency services were fully stretched. After the war, Boots used the building as a garage before converting it into offices. This building was demolished to make way for the National Ice Centre, revealing the remains of many bodies buried here in the nineteenth century.

The birthplace in Notintone Place on 10 April 1829 of William Booth, the founder of the Salvation Army. The house on the left of this picture was in a row of similar properties and was bought by the Salvation Army in the 1930s. After the demolition of the remainder of the terrace these houses were incorporated into an Eventide Home and Goodwill Centre which opened in 1971. In the second photograph Commissioner Catherine Bramwell-Booth, aged eighty-nine, is addressing the crowd after she had unveiled the statue of her grandfather – General Booth – at the opening of the complex. The statue, in typical stance, is a copy of the original at the Salvation Army's training college in Denmark Hill, London.

The London Road High Level Railway Station in 1935. The Great Northern Railway Company built this station at the same time as the Victoria Railway Station but apart from excursion and football trains it was little used. In the 1920s and 1930s Sunday school outings to Radcliffe-on-Trent would begin here and the station would have given the thrill of a major railway terminus to the children. The railway closed for passenger traffic in 1967 and the bridge over London Road was demolished in 1978. Boots warehouses in the background were to remain longer, being pulled down in 1996. In the foreground is the Nottingham Canal flowing towards the River Trent. New buildings are now being erected on the

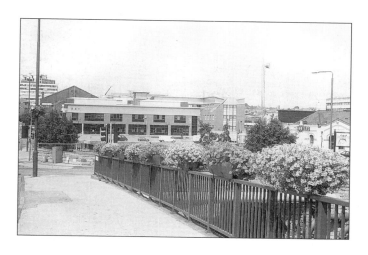

Boots Island Street site, the one in the later photograph is the BBC Centre. The High Level Railway Station booking hall is now Hooters, a bar and restaurant.

Boots printing works and shop stationery department, Station Street, in the 1930s. Jesse Boot began his own printing works in Island Street in the 1890s but, with the expansion of his business, larger premises were required and at the beginning of the twentieth century he took over this factory. It was to become the largest private printing works in the country. In the German blitz on Nottingham in 1941 this building was almost completely destroyed and Thomas Forman & Son took on part of Boots printing for the duration of the war. The new printing works to replace the old one was completed in 1949 and was faced in Portland stone. Boots moved their printing business to Colwick in 1993 and in 1998 Capital One, a credit card company, opened their offices here.

Turney Bros leather works at Trent Bridge in 1952. The tannery opened here in 1861 when John and Edward Turney, who already owned a leather business in Lincoln, began trading here. These works were built in 1911-13 and manufacturing continued until 1981. The workmen in the foreground are erecting a sign advertising the Bath and West Show to be held at Wollaton Park. This was only the second occasion the show had been held in Nottingham; the first time was in 1905. Lorries of two well-known Nottingham firms are approaching Trent Bridge: the Albion on the right belonged to Simms, Sons & Cooke, builders, and to the left is a Leyland truck of John Player & Son.

Today, the leather works have been converted into luxury homes and the remainder of the site is occupied by mews-style houses.

The Midlands Industrial Exhibition, Trent Bridge, in 1903. The main building in Indian style was devoted to exhibits from around the world with Africans, Arabs, Indians and many other races showing their wares. There was also a funfair with a Canadian water chute, a Mexican toboggan and a fairy river. Other attractions included a maze, a biograph pavilion, concert hall, Japanese tea house and a high wire walker. Unfortunately, the fair remained for only a year before being burnt down in July 1904. On the left of the exhibition is A.J. Witty's boathouse and on the far left is the boathouse of the Nottingham Rowing Club. The club, which is the oldest in Nottingham as it was founded in 1862, later merged with the Nottingham Union Rowing Club. In the recent photograph the boathouse on the left belongs to the Nottingham Boat Club. The building on the right was originally the Bridgford Hotel, constructed in 1964 and later became offices of the Rushcliffe Borough Council, although the top floors are now apartments.

The tollhouse at Wilford Bridge in 1958. Construction of the bridge began in 1863 but it was not completed until 1870 due to lack of finance. During this period, a temporary wooden bridge over the River Trent was used by foot passengers and horses. The charges made for vehicles and animals are written on the toll board on the side of the house. Sixpence was charged for every horse or beast drawing a carriage, fourpence for every horse drawing a cart and a penny for every ass carrying more than one person. The bridge was closed to motor traffic in 1974, as it was unsafe, and closed to all traffic in 1981 when it was demolished and rebuilt. The tollhouse, which has several rooms under the arches of the bridge, has now been converted into a newsagent and confectionery shop.

A country cottage in Glapton Lane, Clifton, in 1952. This was the year in which the village was incorporated into Nottingham. The village of Clifton attracted Nottingham folk through the nineteenth and early twentieth centuries – a walk along Clifton Grove would perhaps be followed by tea at one of the cottages on the green. Within two years of the earlier photograph this scene had changed out all of recognition when the Corporation built the largest council house estate in the country here. Stanesby Rise, the road in the modern photograph, is on the site of the old Glapton Lane – the bridle path leading to the main Nottingham road.

The laundry room in the Convent of Mercy, College Street, *c.* 1900. Girls are ironing bedlinen and above them racks of underclothes are hanging to air. The convent was founded in 1844 at premises in Parliament Street and moved to College Street two years later, the same year St Catherine's School for day and boarding pupils was opened. The heyday of the convent was in the 1950s when there were over forty nuns in the community. St Catherine's Grammar School moved from College Street to Aspley in 1962 when it became the Loreto Grammar School. The Sisters of Mercy opened a nursing home in the old school premises in 1990 but

Chapter 5
WORK AND
LEISURE

with the decline in residents and lack of new entrants into the order, the nursing home and the convent both closed in 1999.

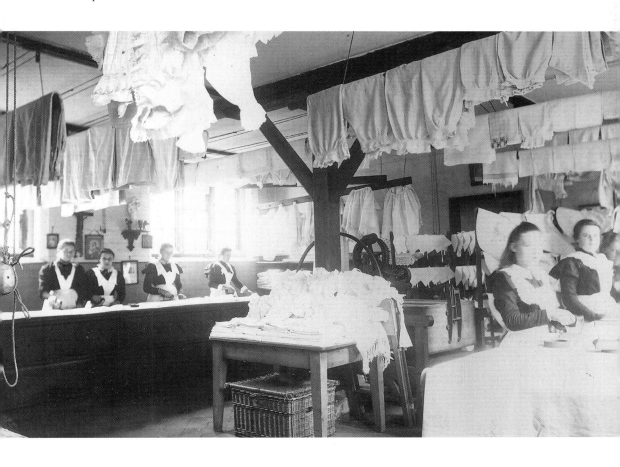

Boots Typists' Training Bureau in 1936. This was the era of shorthand typists who aspired to become secretaries. The bureau was opened in 1935 to teach young employees shorthand and typewriting. The gramophone in the background played music with a beat, such as the William Tell Overture, to encourage rhythm and speed in the typists. The department continued until 1984 when the demand for shorthand typists declined. Today in Boots new D.90 building all staff are computer literate with keyboards and screens at all workstations.

A civic visit to the Castle Telephone Exchange, Broad Street, in 1966. Mrs W. Derbyshire, the Lady Mayoress, listens to June Wheat the telephone operator answering a query from a caller. The first Nottingham exchange opened in Bottle Lane in 1881 when the National Telephone Company began with only two subscribers. The GPO began operating in 1888 and took over completely in 1912 when the private companies were nationalized. In 1928 an automatic exchange for local calls began operating but it was not until 1962 that Subscriber Trunk Dialling for long-distance calls began. Nowadays communication by mobile phone is possible from almost any situation. The 1999 photograph shows Claire Hulland, a customer adviser with the Nottingham Building Society, receiving a call on Cheapside.

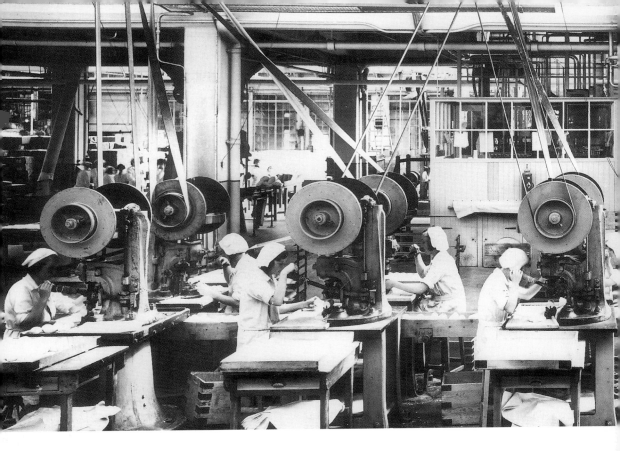

Girls working on soap tablet machines at Boots new factory in Beeston, in 1928. Until the 1920s all Boots factories and warehouses were in Nottingham, centred around London Road in numerous buildings. It had been Jesse Boot's ambition to build a completely new factory site such as Cadbury's at Bournville and Lever's at Port Sunlight. Ill health, however, forced him to give up control of the company and it was left to his son, John Boot, to fulfil his ambition. In the 1930s two landmark factories designed by Sir Owen Williams were built. These were almost completely automated and ahead of their time. Today all Boots factories have state-of-the-art machinery – this 1999 production line is filling hairspray containers.

omen of the Auxiliary Territorial Service sorting mail at the Army Post Office in Nottingham in 1941. All letters, postcards and parcels addressed to the Army went through this sorting office – each week $3\frac{1}{4}$ million letters and 60,000 parcels and packages were dispatched, with the sorting performed entirely by hand. Various locations in the city were used by the Army Post Office including Viyella House, Castle Boulevard and Trent Bridge cricket ground. The Royal Mail's sorting office at Beeston is ultra-modern with automatic handling machines. The Integrated Mail Processor in the later picture differentiates between envelopes and packets, cancels the stamps and sorts first and second-class mail. From this machine the mail is passed to electronic recognition machines which check the addresses against a database and stamp the envelopes with a phosphorescent barcode, enabling them to be sorted into geographical areas.

Workmen walking nonchalantly on the roof of the Nottingham Ice Stadium in 1939, the year in which it was opened. The stadium was built on land cleared of condemned houses around Barker Gate but the outbreak of the Second World War prevented its full use for several years. In 1946 the Nottingham Panthers ice-hockey team was formed and under their coach Sandy Archer, and later Archie Stinchcombe, played exciting matches here. In recent years a new team has been formed attracting large crowds. The stadium saw the emergence of the ice dance pair – Jayne Torvill and Christopher Dean who went on to win world and Olympic titles. Their success encouraged the authorities to build the National Ice Centre in Nottingham on the site of the old Ice Stadium. The new building is shown here nearing completion – the workmen on the roof all wearing hard hats. The tower blocks in the background are the council flats at the bottom of Sneinton Road.

A burst water main on Upper Parliament Street in 1944. The Water Board workmen, having dug a hole, are without exception standing motionless – perhaps discussing their next move. The spectators on the left, including two policemen, are surveying the roadworks which have apparently closed the south side of Parliament Street. The group of workmen in the modern photograph are laying stones near the verge of York Street. Unlike road laying, which is now almost completely automated, laying setts and stones is still a craftsman's job.

Boots firemen with their Leyland fire appliance in the 1930s. These were based at Boots site at Beeston but at the outbreak of the Second World War a unit was formed at the Island Street works. During the blitz on 8 and 9 May 1941 the City Fire Brigade, the Auxiliary Fire Service and the Boots Brigade were fully extended. Bombs fell throughout the city but the majority of the targets were in the city centre and the London Road area. Today, the Boots Fire Brigade has a modern Mercedes appliance and in recent years has had to deal with two major warehouse fires on the Beeston site. In both instances, local fire brigades were called out but the prompt action of the Boots team was of vital importance.

The Nottingham Harmonic Choir and Orchestra with their conductor, Herbert Bardgett, in the Albert Hall in the 1950s. The society was formed in 1856 when the Mechanics Institution Vocal Music Class decided to become a separate entity. In its early years Charles Hallé and Sir Arthur Sullivan were among those associated with the choir. Sir Henry Wood was the principal conductor at the beginning of the twentieth century and other famous conductors who have appeared with the choir were Sir Adrian Boult, Sir Malcolm Sargent and Sir Hamilton Harty. When the Royal Concert Hall was opened in 1982 the choir sang at the inaugural concert and since then have given many fine performances here. The later

photograph is of a dress rehearsal at the concert hall in 1984 conducted by Andrew Burnham with Alex Denman accompanying.

A nostalgic image from the past – platform five at the Midland Railway Station in 1946. The shadows of the iron girders and the travellers transform an ordinary scene into an image of beauty. The dirty pre-war Jubilee locomotive is quietly smoking away while everyone is either waiting for another train or for passengers to arrive. Among the people here are servicemen and women, children, smartly dressed women and a nun. The scene on platform five in 1999 has no romance. The train is the 10.28 a.m. to Cardiff run by Central Trains.

The start of the holidays – travellers waiting with their luggage at the Huntingdon Street bus station in 1964. The majority of holidays were then still taken in Britain, although foreign travel was becoming more popular. Coach travel, although slower than rail was cheaper and the local bus companies ran services to most of the coastal resorts. This bus station, which opened in 1930, was the main coach terminus in the city until 1972 when it was closed and services were transferred to Broad Marsh and the Victoria Centre. The bus station at the former handles traffic to and from the south and here passengers, some with a considerable quantity of luggage, are checking the bus timetables.

A family enjoying their sandwiches in the castle grounds in 1966. The ever-present pigeons feed on any crumbs which fall. In the background is the row of houses on Castle Gate, which in 1974 became the Museum of Costume and Textiles. These houses were built in 1788 for Cornelius Launder, High Sheriff of Nottinghamshire in 1775. In the distance is the Council House, which is no longer visible from this viewpoint. In 1999 a group of schoolgirls from Normandy are sitting in the rain on Edward's Tower, enjoying their lunch with the ubiquitous pigeons for company. Besides improving their English, the girls would no doubt learn why a castle in Nottingham came to be built by a Norman duke.

A sedate scene at the England v West Indies test match at Trent Bridge in 1966. The ground had not seen many changes since the 1930s apart from the electronic scoreboard at the Radcliffe Road and Fox Road corner. The ground capacity was 30,000 but is only half that today as spectators are no longer allowed to encroach onto the grass. The modern Trent Bridge ground is significantly different. Some changes have been made to the pavilion but the greatest alteration has been on the Radcliffe Road side. In 1975 Nottinghamshire County Council built a ten-storey office block in the corner of the ground and in 1998 Trent Bridge, which still hosts test matches, had a new stand built with state-of-the-art facilities for the cricketers and media. The 1999 match is Nottinghamshire v

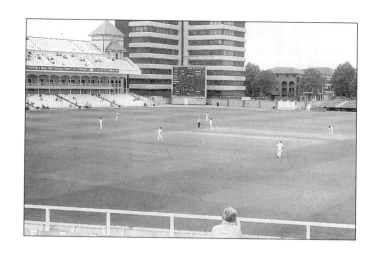

Warwickshire watched by only a handful of spectators. Nottinghamshire needed 132 runs to win but were all out for 76 in their second innings – their worst total for 22 years.

Boys enjoying a spot of fishing in the River Leen at Basford in 1966. This pastime was more popular then than now – to stroll to a nearby lake or stream on a summer's day and to fish with a rod or net was ideal. To catch a fish was not certain but the unpredictability of fishing is part of its charm. Children today, in spite of all the electronic games, still enjoy old-fashioned amusements. The later photograph shows youngsters riding on a roundabout in the Old Market Square.

Teenagers boating on the lake in Highfields Park in 1966. Ever since the park was opened in the 1920s it has been a popular spot for the people of Nottingham. There are plans for a new tearoom to be opened and a walk to be created around the lake. In contrast with the tranquillity of the earlier pastime, white water rafting on a slalom course is hair-raising. These four girls in the charge of a raft-guide are riding the rapids at the Holme Pierrepont Water Sports Centre. The centre was opened in 1973 and also has facilities for rowing, water-skiing and yachting.

Goose Fair in 1925. The 1920s were the last decade that the fair was held in the Market Place. The event was eagerly awaited by townspeople and showmen alike. For ordinary folk the few days of the fair were an escape from the drudgery of everyday living. The shows appeared to promise the wonders of the earth and the latest rides from America made the old favourites such as the galloping horses old-fashioned. On the right are Collins' steam gondolas which were for the brave-hearted. Today's Goose Fair on the Forest makes the old fair seem very tame with the new rides becoming more sensational each year. The big wheel and the helter-skelter, however, still make their annual appearance.

A father and mother with their two daughters on the horses and cockerels roundabout in the 1920s. This sedate ride costing 2d was the roundabout which most families preferred. The gaily-coloured horses and cockerels all had unusual names; this horse was called Ptah. The same ride can still be seen at the present-day fair, giving as much enjoyment as in the past. The music accompanying the ride may not be produced by an organ, but apart from the fare little else has changed.

Children playing in the sand at the Riverside Pleasure Park by the River Trent in 1933. This park was very popular in the summer, approached either down Trent Lane, by pleasure boat from Trent Bridge or by ferry across the river. Deckchairs and parasols could be hired, teas and ice creams purchased and children could play with their buckets and spades at the water's edge. More recently, Nottingham has brought the seaside to the Old Market Square. For a few days each summer, the Corporation turns part of the square into Nottingham-by-the-sea, with a patch of sand and a boardwalk with deckchairs and entertainers. The Old Market Square, which for years had a very formal appearance, is now beginning to acquire a new image.